Art Book

By Almond Tree

Art Book

By Almond Tree

Copyright © 2021 Almond Tree
All rights Reserved
ISBN: 978-1-716-17806-1

Brief notes:

I often (but not always) symbolize God, The Almighty, in the thunderstorm. Living waters are rivers. Rivers come from heaven. God's river is in the heavens, in the clouds, and He directs it where He wills.

The main intention and hope of this book is to draw people back to the stories in the scriptures. I hope to cause an intrigue and desire for people to take another look, and another look, and another look. The depths and heights of these stories are unending. I also hope to open up doors of further insight, that people may begin to see things that I am unable to see. Taking line upon line, to seek out the manifold wisdom that would come to and through a manifold body.

Special Thanks:

I have never studied art, but I have been influenced and inspired by others' work that I greatly admire. I do not think my work holds up in comparison to their's, so I highly suggest that people look at the art of these other artist.

First and foremost, I would like to give thanks to God. All glory be to Him.

I would like to thank Matthew Conner for all the advice and direction he has offered me, and of course, his friendship. I specifically took inspiration from him for the John the Baptist drawing.

I would like to thank my cousin, Chris Schweizer. He is an amazing cartoonist who has given me a lot of advice throughout the years.

And of course, I would like to thank Bill Watterson. I have probably been most influenced by his work. The only books I chose to read growing up are the Bible and Calvin and Hobbes. I like to say they are the two sources of all truth.

THE LAMP

"The lamp of the body is the eye. If therefore your eye is good, your whole body will be full of light. But if your eye is bad, your whole body will be full of darkness. If therefore, the light that is in you is darkenss, how great is that darkness.

Your word is a lamp unto my feet and a light unto my path.

In Your light we see light.

For You will light my lamp; the Lord my God will enlighten my darkness.

Then the kingdom of heaven shall be likend to ten virgins who took their lamps and went out to meet the bridegroom. Now five of them were wise, and five were foolish. Those who were foolish took their lamps and took no oil with them, but the wise took oil in their vessels with their lamps.

And you shall command the children of Israel that they bring you pure oil of pressed olives for the light, to cause the lamp to burn continually.

Watch therefore, for you know neither the day nor hour in which the Son of Man is coming."

Matthew 6:22-23, Psalm 119:105, Psalm 18:28, Psalm 36:9, Matthew 25:1-13, Exodus 27:20

ALMOND BLOSSOM

WATCHMEN

Woe to you, o land, when your king is a child
And your princes feast in the morning
And the men of war are drunk at noon
And the trumpet serves no warning
For a warning, a warning, a war is at hand
For all this they would not hear
Nor shake themselves from a sleep of stupor
Nor incline their ear
They need not a worldly song
That the worlds unfit to use
But enchanted from the heavens
A song that speaks of You
A voice heard behind the ear
"Turn to the right or to the left
This is the highway fit for kings
This is the way, now walk in it"
Let us wear this wisdom as a weapon
It wears not the watcher out
Let us turn the wheel at the well of water
And draw it to our mouths

Watchman, watchman, what do you see?
I see the branch of an almond tree
Ready to blossom, ready to bloom
Watchman, watchman, what of the night?
I see the dawn of the morning light
Bursting from the womb

NEHUSTAN

Numbers 21:6-9

So the Lord sent fiery serpents among the people, and they bit the people; and many of the people of Israel died. Therefore the people came to Moses, and said, "We have sinned, for we have spoken against the Lord and against you; pray to the Lord that He take away the serpents from us." So Moses prayed for the people.

Then the Lord said to Moses, "Make a fiery serpent, and set it on a pole; and it shall be that everyone who is bitten, when he looks at it, shall live." So Moses made a bronze serpent, and put it on a pole; and so it was, if a serpent had bitten anyone, when he looked at the bronze serpent, he lived.

2 Kings 18:4

He removed the high places and broke the sacred pillars, cut down the wooden image and broke in pieces the bronze serpent that Moses had made; for until those days the children of Israel burned incense to it, and called it Nehushtan.

CREEPING THING

Ezekiel 8:10
Romans 1:23

THE FIELD MOUSE

There was a tiny field mouse
Who scurried 'cross the ground
And he crept into my house
For he barely made a sound
Then one night I came across him
And I thought to throw him out
But it was chilly in the evening
So, I let him stick around
He spoke one lonely hour
"I'm not like other mice, you see,
For I carry joy and wisdom
And a gracious company"
I listened to his words
For his words were soft and sweet
And I regarded it as scripture
With no false word or deceit
Soon the mouse had turned to many
Running rampant 'cross my floors
They devoured all my food
Behind every cabinet door

I was helpless as a baby
As they stole candy from my cradle
Thus, I sought for resolution
Be it friendly or it fatal
I laid serpents on my floors
And sent vipers in my walls
Soon the squeaking of the mice
Was never heard at all
But the bites of snakes would fester
Every hour they grew worse
For what came as a solution
Had now become a curse
So, I ran unto the water
Searching for compassion
For pity and for mercy
In any kind of fashion
And as I began to sink
The Christ where love abounds
Took my hand like Peter
And set me back on solid ground

Trust in the Lord with all your heart,
And lean not on your own understanding;
In all your ways acknowledge Him,
And He shall direct your paths. (Proverbs 3:5-6)

RAVEN DOVE

Genesis 8:6-12
Luke 10:5-6

RAVEN DOVE

Hasten not after the ravens
That flutter too and fro
For the dove will bring an olive branch
And lead me where to go
In the quiet, in the night
I heard a voice that spoke to me
"If we all follow the maestro
It makes a perfect symphony"
His breeze blows through the trees
Through the branches, through the leaves
It cheers me on, it lifts my heart
And it brings me to my knees
Put my whole world in perspective
Just how small the biggest is
Everything will come and go
With the passing of the wind
Teach the number of my days
And cause me to know my end
That I may gain a heart of wisdom
To know how frail I am

I dipped my finger in the honey
And I fell into the pot
No more grasping at the wind
Trying to get what I have got
I will not set my mind
On all that which is not
For riches come and go
Riches surely come and go
From the belly of the eater
There came something to eat
From the belly of the strong
There came something sweet
Give me the milk and the honey
Give me the meat
For I desire to grow
Skin for skin and dust to dust
A flower fades and dies
Vanity of vanities
A futile state of mind
But the honey never spoils
And light forever shines
I will follow it home
We break the bread and drink the wine
A time and times and half a time
To the ones to come, what can I leave behind?
I will bake a little cake before I go

THE RIDDLE
Judges chapter 14

"If you had not plowed with my heifer,
You would not have solved my riddle!"

ASAHEL — 2 Samuel 2:18-23 / Habakuk 3:19 — "And Asahel was as fleet of foot as a wild gazelle. The LORD God is my strength; He will make my feet like deer's feet, And He will make me walk on my high hills. To the Chief Musician. With my stringed instruments."

STEPHEN THE MARTYR

Acts chapter 7

"I desire mercy and not sacrifice"

Yet, the sacrifice of Stephen's life would spread abroud His mercy.
"This is a faithful saying and worthy of all acceptance, that Christ Jesus came into the world to save sinners, of whom I am chief. Therefore I say to you, her sins, which are many, are forgiven, for she loved much. But to whom little is forgiven, the same loves little."
And so to see ourselves as chief sinners causes mercy to futher grow.

BEERSHEBA — GENESIS 21:28-33
WELL OF THE OATH. WELL OF THE SEVEN.

"You will take seven ewe lambs from my hand, that they may be my witness that i have dug this well."

THE BUTLER AND THE BAKER

Genesis chapter 40

"Do not interpretations belong to God?"

DEN OF LIONS

"My God sent His angel and shut the lions' mouths, so that they have not hurt me, because I was found innocent before Him; and also, O king, I have done no wrong before you."

"He makes his angels spirits, His ministers a flame of fire"

Daniel chapter 6

~BAPTISMS~

BAPTISIMS

Moses and Joshua

Through the red sea,
Into the wilderness.
Through the Jordan,
Into the promised land.

Exodus 14:22, Joshua 4:23, Genesis 1:7, Hebrews 4:14, 1 Corinthians 10:2

"Thus God made the firmament, and divided the waters which were under the firmament from the waters which were above the firmament; and it was so."

Out of Egypt, the house of bondage, through the red sea, into the wilderness.

"all were baptized into Moses in the cloud and in the sea."

"Seeing then that we have a great High Priest who has passed through the heavens, Jesus the Son of God, let us hold fast our confession."

The Jordan river, that river in the sky.
Living waters. Flowing waters.
Rivers from and in the heavens.

PHARAOH

Pharaoh, where is all the fruit
We once dipped in honey and molasses?
To celebrate our youth
While the angel passes
Have you seen your eldest son?
He's in the courtyard dying
I hear mourning in the morning
From all the mothers crying
On the legs of royal horses
Through the fields of grain
Pharaoh, I will take my fruit
When we go our separate ways
The waters split and stand upright
And give us favor as we go
Hell and heartache close behind
Yet the sea swallows them whole
Do I eat the bread of heaven?
Angels food come from above?
Yet still pursue that milk and honey
And a sweetness on my tongue
I will wander through the sands
Through a vast and barren land
I'll be buried with my faith
Under this rock on which I stand
I heard of grapes and wine to swallow
From the vineyard of my dreams
Yet there's an idol that I follow
And a friendship that I leave
Strike that stone and give me water
Oh, but Moses, I want wine
The Blood that brings me to my Father
Saying "rest you child of mine"

It tastes like honey on my lips
It feels like aloe to my skin

JAEL (Meaning "mountain goat")   Judges 4:17-22
Judges 5:24-27

"Most blessed among women is Jael, the wife of Heber the Kenite; blessed is she among women in tents. He asked for water, she gave milk; she brought out cream in a lordly bowl."

MAN OF GOD

1 Kings chapter 13

"the lion had not eaten the corpse nor torn the donkey"

FLATTERY vs. TRUTH

Ezekiel 13:10, Isaiah 59:14-15, Daniel 11:32

Truth, like a lion, does not back down from anything, and it will tear to pieces, and we don't always like it. Yet flattery will choke the life out of truth; proclaiming "peace, peace", when there is not peace. We are not okay in our sins, we are pursuing destrucion. Repent, all of us. "Return to Me", says the Lord.

"Justice is turned back, And righteousness stands afar off; For truth has fallen in the street, And equity cannot enter. So truth fails, And he who departs from evil makes himself a prey."

GHOST SAMUEL — "An old man is coming up, and he is covered with a mantle." — 1 Samuel 28:3-25

VULTURES
Genesis 15:11, Matthew 24:28, Luke 17:37

"And when the vultures came down on the carcasses, Abram drove them away."

"The goat on which the lot fell for Azazel shall be presented alive before the LORD to make atonement over it, that it may be sent away into the wilderness to Azazel. Aaron shall lay both his hands on the head of the live goat, confess over it all the iniquities of the children of Israel, and all their transgressions, concerning all their sins, putting them on the head of the goat, and shall send it away into the wilderness by the hand of a suitable man. The goat shall bear on itself all their iniquities to an uninhabited land; and he shall release the goat in the wilderness."

YOM KIPPUR

"It shall be to you a sabbath of solemn rest, and you shall afflict your souls."

Leviticus chapter 16 and 23:26-32

THE THINNEST WEEDS

There were the thinnest weeds growing through the garden
I tore them from their roots
There were the smallest words calling greatest caution
That echoed through the room
Why would I beg and plead for things that which are mine,
Declaring lies the higher truth?
Catch for us the little foxes that spoil all the vines
For our vineyard is in bloom

Jesus Christ, where is your bride to be
Debating eschatology?
Entangled in theology?
She forgot to fall in love

I find that all the blind are those who claim to see
And who traverse the universe have yet to stand on feet
Yet we sit up in the heavens and proclaim our royalty
But the brightest of the stars will fall like apples from a tree

You've never met a lover like me
Such a lover of things
All my fields are cursed with curs
And overgrown with weeds

"Son of David, have mercy on me"

CROWN OF THORNS

Mark 4:18-19

SWORD OF GOLIATH *"There is none like it; give it to me."* 1 Samuel 21:8-9

"Mercy and truth have met together; Righteousness and peace have kissed."

LION AND LAMB
Psalm 85:10

Truth and mercy. The son of David. Righteousness and peace. The son of Solomon. King and priest. Melchizedek. The Lion of Judah. The Lamb of God.

Exodus 3:14, Ecclesiastes 3:11
"He has put eternity in their hearts"

LOGOS OF LIFE

Logos, Truth, Reason, Meaning, Essence, Origin, Purpose
The I AM from which all things are.

CALL TO ME

Drawn away from uptown pleasures and all the city lights
To plant my roots among the stars beneath the mountain sky
The handiwork of heaven crafted marvelously in place
I hear an echo in the night that beckons to my name

    Call to me
    I'm calling back
    I'm ready to be going
    Call to me
    I'm calling back
    I'm ready to be gone

To ride upon the wings of time and lose all sense of home
To become another passerby who has given all to hope
As memories would dance like devils with curses on their breath
Til past and present meet the future to resurrect the dead

    Call to me
    I'm calling back
    I'm ready to be going
    Call to me
    I'm calling back
    I'm ready to be gone

Did I ever know the Sabbath, did I ever know a rest?
I saw time much like a line with a beginning and an end
Yet it worked itself in circles beyond what could be known
And many birds have sung their songs 'bout dusty trail and open road

    Call to me
    I'm calling back
    I'm ready to be going
    Call to me
    I'm calling back
    I'm ready to be gone

CHERUB   EZEKIEL CHAPTER 1   "Each one had four faces,
                               EZEKIEL 10:7   and each one had four wings."

~ EDEN ~
Genesis chapter 2

"And Adam called his wife's name Eve, because she was the mother of all living." ~ EVE ~ Genesis 3:20

LOBOTOMY

If you decide to inscribe my theories in books
Write it down with vanishing ink
There's a difference between my lobotomy
And consuming one too many drinks
I don't want to remember what's mine anymore
I only want thoughts drawn from you
For the home that I once tried to make for myself
Began to swallow me up as a tomb
I held my loved one and watched her depart
And sorrow rolled in like a cloud
But liquors for losers and not broken hearts
And my face doesn't favor a frown
If I'm hungry for fruit I must first grow the tree
And my heart is turned over and tilled
I gave up the grape that my tongue might be clean
For my mind to find strength and be filled
Yet heaven was silent and God disappeared
As sorrow was testing my heart
The sinking, the swimming, the walking on water
As I end where the Lord takes His start
I see years teaching ears to be open and listening
So repetition will say it again
Liquors a liar for weak hearted sissies
Masquerading as though it's a friend

There's no life in all of my living
There's no strength in the strength of a man
When having it all turns to nothing
Mercy brings my world to an end

MERCY

What did we come out to see
A reed shaken by the wind?
As magical as God may be
He is not a magic trick
We speak with pride upon our lips
And the chatter of a fool
But shall God converse with donkeys
Or take communion with a mule?
Can this tongue praise God above
While it exalts the name of Pharaoh?
Who can wield a wooden sword
Or shoot a crooked arrow?
Rip the womb wide open
And dash my baby on the rocks
If I've conceived deceit and lies
And evil in my thoughts
Mary, Mary, mother of all
Do you sit as His right hand?
If I may request of thee
That I might come before the Lamb
So that my shaky legs may break
And I might fall upon my face
And plead for mercy
Have mercy on me

In truth, does it endure forever?
Where the seven turns into eight?
The infinite calls to my heart
And beckons to my name
And how could I live if I never forgive?
Have mercy, have mercy on me

SLEEP AND SLUMBER

A little sleep, a little slumber
A little dream, a little wonder
A little folding of the hands to sleep
I am earth and solid ground
And just another hand me down
Blade to flower, fruit to death, return to seed
All of us are everlasting
To come again with winter's passing
The memories of joy that came through grief
I took the coin and slayed the lamb
Yet I cannot save a single man
And dare not try to save myself from me

MOUNT CARMEL

1 KINGS 18:20-40

ELIJAH - My God is Lord

EGYPT, ASSYRIA, BABYLON
SPIRITUAL KINGDOMS

1 Samuel 16:7 "the Lord does not see as man sees; for man looks at the outward appearance, but the Lord looks at the heart."
What is the character and nature of the kingdom? What is its logos? What is its purpose, its reason, its essence?

EGYPT:

The House of Bondage.
Galatians 4:24 "which gives birth to bondage, which is Hagar"
Fleshly kingdom. Earthly and carnal. Materialism. Placing trust and confidence in the work of our hands.
The contrast: Deuteronomy 11:10-11, Egypt vs Canaan, the house of bondage vs the land of promise, toil vs rest.
She is the kingdom that we go to when the heavens are shut up and there is a famine in the land. She offers bread and provision. Yet, after a time, she forgets Joseph, and we find ourselves bound.
She is the cruel stepmother.
She is a broken reed. She is not the strength of our hope and trust.
Ezekiel 29:7 "Egypt has been a staff of reed to the house of Israel. When they took hold of you with the hand, you broke and tore all their shoulders; when they leaned on you, you broke and made all their backs quiver."

ASSYRIA:

Kingdom of oppression, affliction, persecution and tribulation.
Rod of wrath (Isaiah 10:5)
Consumes like the locust (Nahum 3:17)
Devours like lions (Nahum 2:11-12)
Causes fear and tries to get one to deny God.
2 Chronicles 32:18 "…to frighten them and trouble them, that they might take the city."
Isaiah 37:15 "Do not let Hezekiah make you trust in the Lord, saying, 'The Lord will surely deliver us.'"

TYRE:

Kingdom of merchant ships that transfer the riches and wealth of this world. The world's counterfeit bread, gold, silver, vineyards, olive groves and fig trees. She is not necessarily a wealthy kingdom, but a kingdom that transfers the flow of wealth. A land of trade. The great merchant city. The harlot who sits on many waters. The siren who sits in the midst of the seas. Seas of peoples, nations, multitudes and tongues.

BABYLON:

Kingdom of pride and selfishness.
Kingdom of confusion, deceit and deception.
1 John 2:16 "all that is in the world—the lust of the flesh, the lust of the eyes, and the pride of life."
The tower of Babel. Mankind exalting himself to the heavens. Mankind as God. 666, the number of man.
Daniel 3:1, "Nebuchadnezzar the king made an image of gold, whose height was sixty cubits and its width six cubits"

MEDES/PERSIANS:

They don't regard gold or silver (Isaiah 13:17).
Their word does not alter (Daniel 6:8, 6:12).
They conquered Babylon.
Why?
They value words. They value integrity and honesty. They value these more than money, pleasures, and the fleeting riches of this life.
They don't take bribes (Exodus 23:8, Deuteronomy 10:17 & 16:19)

BODY DIVIDED BODY TOGETHER

BODY DIVIDED
Matthew 5:30 "And if your right hand causes you to sin, cut it off and cast it from you; for it is more profitable for you that one of your members perish, than for your whole body to be cast into hell."
Judges 19:29-30 "When he entered his house he took a knife, laid hold of his concubine, and divided her into twelve pieces, limb by limb, and sent her throughout all the territory of Israel. And so it was that all who saw it said, 'No such deed has been done or seen from the day that the children of Israel came up from the land of Egypt until this day. Consider it, confer, and speak up!' "

BODY TOGETHER
Judges 20:1 and 11 "So all the children of Israel came out, from Dan to Beersheba, as well as from the land of Gilead, and the congregation gathered together as one man before the Lord at Mizpah. So all the men of Israel were gathered against the city, united together as one man."
Ezekiel 37:7-10 "So I prophesied as I was commanded; and as I prophesied, there was a noise, and suddenly a rattling; and the bones came together, bone to bone. Indeed, as I looked, the sinews and the flesh came upon them, and the skin covered them over; but there was no breath in them. Also He said to me, "Prophesy to the breath, prophesy, son of man, and say to the breath, 'Thus says the Lord God: "Come from the four winds, O breath, and breathe on these slain, that they may live." ' " So I prophesied as He commanded me, and breath came into them, and they lived, and stood upon their feet, an exceedingly great army."

Our sister Sodom, more righteous.
Judges 19
Genesis 19:1-29
Little Benjamin, he justifies our sister Sodom. How often that we do the same.
Ezekiel 16:46-52
"Look, the sin of Sodom was that they had pride, fullness of food, and abundance of idleness; neither did they strengthen the hand of the poor and needy."
It will be more tolerable in the day of judgement for Sodom than for us.
Matthew 11:24

I find this story in Judges very intriguing, especially the similarities and differences when compared to the Genesis story. I don't feel that I have understanding on it yet, not even to a small degree. Above are just some thoughts and links to other scriptures that came to mind.

Compare and contrast Genesis 19 and Judges chapters 19-21

Sidenote: Benjamin means "son of my right hand", yet the Benjamites are often described as being left-handed.

"What do you mean sleeper? Arise, call on your God." **SHIP TO TARSHISH** Jonah chapter 1

"Out of the belly of sheol I cried, And You heard my voice."

BELLY OF SHEOL

Jonah chapter 2

"Now the word of the Lord came to Jonah the second time."

SHORES OF NINEVEH

Jonah chapter 3

"You had pity on the plant, And should I not pity Nineveh?"

PLANT OF PITY

Jonah chapter 4

THE WILLOWS

We hung our harps on the willows
With weeping and wailing for the mountains
My heart shall wail like flutes for you
Like flutes my heart shall wail
My city of peace, my upmost joy
I sit lowly in the dust
Like a dove my heart shall moan for you
My heart shall moan like a dove

How can I sing the Lord's song as I live in a foreign land?
My comfort and correction come both from the same hand
If I forget you, O Jerusalem, let my hand forget its skill
Yet my bones hope for salvation, as my eyes lift to the hills
By the rivers of captivity, I sit down on foreign banks
O my soul, why are you cast down?
My soul, march on in strength
Though all my sighs are many
And my heavy heart is faint
O my soul, don't be cast down
My soul, march on in strength
To behold the harp of hearts
And pluck upon strings
Echo through the dark
And upward to the king
My tongue, the pen of a writer
His precious blood, the ink
O, the blood of the Lamb, the sweetest thing
Let it ever come to me

WOOD AND METAL

Fields of grain and endless travel
Where skyline met the rivers end
This railroad laid of wood and metal
Could lead me to my love again
Coins laid on the track to flatten
As the cars keep rolling by
I take the time I wish I hadn't
To watch my shadow leave my side

I was once a poor man
I was once a rich man
I was once a young man with no care
I once had many friends
I once had many lovers
But I gave it all to get there

Fields of grain and endless travel
And a book for when I'm lost
I was saved with wood and metal
And a Friend hung on a cross

THE SWEETEST WINE

The blood of Jesus Christ
Tastes like the sweetest wine
But how much more when I
Am pressed to death
The weeping at the walls
I watch the city fall
The strongest of them all
Asleep in bed
I built my heart like Jericho
Guarding all my precious things
Complacency took hold of me
In the season of the spring
Eat and drink and raise the glass
All my princes proclaimed peace
Yet my pleasures that once gave me joy
Have now become my enemies
The King rose up to tear me down
Bringing the mercy of the sword
To shred my heart as strings of harps
And pluck out every chord
It echoes through my empty soul
With the cooing of the doves
Where truth and mercy interweave
And resonate in love

Pour the wine
Break the bread
The oil running down His head
This is for His burial
This is for His death
Spill the blood
Tear the flesh
Enter through into Your rest
This is for our burial
This is for our death

CROSSES

The footprints of the flock have led me through this death
I watch the floodplain rise and flow over my head
I took sorrow as my servant, I took sorrow as my slave
For my weeping worked humility and brought me to my grave
For all the world could offer has slipped out of my hands
As if everything I held was only tiny grains of sand
The futility of life brought forth the sanity of mind
And the valley of this darkness has now given birth to light
So I look toward the heavens and I come unto these terms
That there will come a day when there is no more wick to burn
The wise have eyes inside the head, but the fool looks to the earth
So I find that I must die to reconcile my new birth
For I see crosses on the hill, hanging every type of man
The blasphemer, the repentant, and the sacrificial lamb
There was crucified a Savior, yet there remains a cross for me
Take the world and give me Jesus, He is everything I need

"Surely you are a husband of blood to me! You are a husband of blood!"

HUSBAND OF BLOOD

RED

"With moisture He saturates the thick clouds, and they swirl about, being turned by His guidance." RIVER OF GOD BLUE

"So he waited yet another seven days and sent out the dove, which did not return again to him anymore"

DOVE OF NOAH

PURPLE

RED BLUE PURPLE

These are thoughts and ideas still in process.

Red - earth, blood, flesh, Moses, the law, structure, mother, house, country, garden
Blue - heaven, water, Elijah, the prophets, father, tradition, knowledge, intelligence
Purple - Spirit, anointing. Noah's dove (not as a definite symbolic image, but because the Holy Spirit is sometimes symbolized as a dove. Also, I personally referenced purple as a dove because of the first mention to the olive tree in Genesis), logos, king, the fear of the Lord
These three, interwoven, provide a veil for one to pass through, furthering their proximity into God's presence, into the Holiest.
These three make the union and manifest the Kingdom of Heaven, the Kingdom of God. They manifest wisdom and life.

HUSBAND OF BLOOD
Exodus 4:24-26
Red, Earth, Flesh, Blood, Moses, the Law
1st Birth, 1st Baptism

RIVER OF GOD
Psalm 65:9-10, Job 37:11-13
Blue, Heaven, Water, Elijah, the Prophets
2nd Birth, 2nd Baptism

DOVE OF NOAH
Matthew 3:11 & 16, John 1:33, Isaiah 61:1, Luke 4:18, Acts 10:38, 1 John 2:20
Spirit, Anointing
3rd Birth, 3rd Baptism
1 John 5:6-8

"This is He who came by water and blood—Jesus Christ; not only by water, but by water and blood. And it is the Spirit who bears witness, because the Spirit is truth. For there are three that bear witness in heaven: the Father, the Word, and the Holy Spirit; and these three are one. And there are three that bear witness on earth: the Spirit, the water, and the blood; and these three agree as one."
Drawing near, closer to the the Holiest, and passing through three colors: Red, Blue, and Purple
Exodus 26:31 (the veil), 29:4 (water), 29:21 (blood and anointing oil)
To be born of blood, then of water, then of Spirit. This pattern stacks up and parallels throughout all scripture and reality. To go through Moses, Elijah, to Jesus. The law, the prophets, to the Son of God. The Red Sea, the Jordan, to the land of promise. We see this in ourselves. We see this in Jesus (John 1:13, 26, & 33, John 3:5). We see this in the beginning: Genesis 1:1-2, the heavens (blue), the earth (red), and the Dove, the Holy Spirit (purple).

BLOOD AND WATER

You've broken all my bones and put them in the boil
And ladle out what's left of me upon the dusty soil
The dirt is red
The earth is red
From the blood that fills her cup
The sky is blue
Holding the waters
That could wash this world of lust
And when the two agree
I see a glimpse of royalty
As a princely price that's placed upon my days
As the blending turns to purple
Every obstacle and hurdle
Becomes a strength

The blood and the waters
My conscience is clear
My unworthiness
Caused me to draw near
My spirit is broken
That the Spirit might come
Descending with olives
And the wings of a dove

SUFFER THE LOSS OF ALL THINGS

My face is set for the journey
With the sandals on my feet
May I partake of Your sufferings,
And suffer the loss of all things
The work of a skillful lamenter
Let me bow down my head
Being conformed to Your image
As I'm being conformed to Your death
The root has extended its branches
And my head has risen too high
So lop off the bough in Your mercy
And cut off the horn of my pride
For I am small in all of my greatness
But in smallness I seem to be great
And through Your grace I find all my weakness
That I might find all Your strength

The earth and the heavens shook to and fro
And fear had replaced what my mind seem to know
As my little star falls down from the sky
Where am I left at the end of the night?
Oh, how all the gold has lost every glimmer
The worlds growing fat as I'm growing thinner
My flesh on Your altar, my heart in Your peace
My guestroom kept furnished, empty and clean
For if You are my Father, then where is Your honor?
If You are Almighty, then where is my dread?
If You are my King, then let me bow down
And fall at Your feet as though I was dead
If You are my Potter, then let me be molded
If You are my river, let me drown in Your love
If You are my Savior, then I give You my life
That You'd give me Your death, and resurrect us in One

PHILISTINE LORDS

1 Samuel chapters 5 and 6

There is a way that the merchandise of this world corresponds to sea. The way that the wealth of this world flows like rivers into a sea of peoples.

There is a siren song of money, and the merchandise of this world calls out to us. There are sailors who traverse the waves of the sea, and the waves of the wealth of the world. And yet, to become distracted by the sirens' song will only lead to our demise. Our ships will be dashed to pieces upon the rocks, as the sirens drag us down to the depths.

The Philistines are a people who dwell by the sea. Could these be a people who dwell closely to the desires of the wealth of the world? Creeping sea rats, seeking after whatever crumbs they can gather?

Who is this great fish, this god Dagon, that these sea rats worship? Do they worship this great being that swims through the waves of the sea? A great being that knows it's waters well? A great fish that knows the flowing of the wealth of the world?

THE CITY BY THE SEA

Every soul sails to and fro
In ships on seas of pleasure
The merchandise comes at a price
And time is bound to treasure
I sell my soul and pay the toll
To become a god of weather
Yet the sea does not give birth to me
But swallows beyond measure

There is something in the deep
That shakes below my feet
That bellows from the darkness
And beckons unto me
Leviathan will play
And thrash beneath the waves
Death glories at his day
As he dances on my grave

Who can live beside the sea
And not be broken by it?
What man does she not dash against the rocks?
I wasn't meant to live here darling
I was made for tending gardens
I was made to plant and farm the crops

FISHERS OF MEN

"He spoke all things in parables", for types and shadows and symbols and patterns. Yet seeing, they might not see, and hearing, they might not hear. I too was once like a fish, flowing with the current of the waves, swimming in a world of darkness, and without a solid foundation to stand upon. I followed the sway of the sea, seeking the things of the world, gold and silver, food and clothing, riches and wealth. Yet a dart pierced my heart, killed me, and caused me to live again, no longer as a creature of the sea. We wrestle not against flesh and blood, but we fight against those dark and twisted words and ideas that are spewed from the mouth of the leviathan. We divide the light from the darkness, and the truth from the lie, piercing the heart of pride and self righteousness. If Christ died, then we are all dead. All need mercy. All need saving. Like fishers of men, we pull up from the sea, and as they gasp and flop on the deck, we present the breath of life that they are dying for.

Mystery of Babylon the great, the mother of harlots; and her whore daughter is making sweet melody to all those who dwell in the earth. Tyre built for herself a tower, heaped up silver like the dust, and gold like the mire of the streets. She sat at the entrance of the sea. A merchant of all the peoples. A city of sirens. How the wealth of the world and all its merchandise calls out and sings to us. All the ships to Tarshish and Sidon are dashed against the rocks. The sea does not give birth or bear children.

There is no life in her, and her desire is to drown you. Money cannot purchase a moment, or lengthen a day of our lives. Death approaches, and time will cut us down at the feet, and the head of Babylon will fall.

"Turn away my eyes from looking at worthless things."

Let us not become distracted by distractions, or by the roaring and the noise of the waves.

We cannot walk on water without Jesus Christ as Lord.

Matthew 4:19, Habakkuk 1:14 — FISHERS OF MEN — "Why do you make men like fish of the sea, Like creeping things that have no ruler over them?"

Zechariah 4:2-3 and 11-14, Two olive trees
Romans 11, Isaiah 43:12, Acts 1:8, Israel and the Church

TWO WITNESSES

Romans 3:21, The law and the prophets
Matthew 17:3, Mark 9:4, Luke 9:30, Moses and Elijah

THE DOGS BED

Our wellness resides
In where the dog lies
And where doth he lie?
Where doth he lie?
To thirst on the street in the late summer heat
As the pangs in the belly turn bitter to sweet
Or tied to a stump and left alone
Cursed to wander with nowhere to roam
Without shelter or bed
Or roof overhead
Living year after year
With a rope 'round the neck
In the long winter night
To succumb to the bite
Of the frost and the cold
As the wind whistles 'round about 'round his bones

Our wellness resides
In where the dog lies
And where doth he lie?
Where doth he lie?
Yet the entire desire the heart's longing after
Is to acquire a place at the feet of the master
Yet we walk by and by
And push all aside
But if we were wise to open our eyes
We would give ourselves back
And pine for the pack
And we too might go howl at the moon

RACHEL

Elijah came in with a sword to my soul
To cut open this psyche I couldn't control
The voice said "cry out", yet what shall I cry?
"That all flesh is grass and all men must die"
Yet all men are seeking a runaway bride
A runaway bride they do not recognize
The complacent consume her and cast her aside
The distracted devour her limbs and her eyes
Yet a war ensues at the end of the road
As she takes up her sword to the substance of hope
And she dashes to pieces a future of dreams
Yet eternity tears her apart at the seams
She's gracious and cruel, I can't comprehend
If she comes near to me as a foe or a friend
Yet she goes on unloved, a life of disdain
Unveiling her value at the door or death's gate
Then all men go seeking this runaway bride
For time is a mistress they cannot entice

Now wisdom came out with a yoke and a plow
To lengthen my furrows and turn up my ground
For to number my days would prove me to be wise
As my star fades away and my hours slip by
For love wasn't quite as light as they said
But came with a burden I didn't expect
Nor did I reject
But learned to respect
As a portion of bread that I must accept

To take and break and eat and swallow it down

How does my heart keep walking
Without you by my side?
For I've lost a light that burned
In the darkest of my nights
We never made it home together
We never made it home
You died along the road
And we never made it home

The tears were sown at Luz
I set a pillar by your grave
Rachel, my Rachel
Buried on the way

THE ALMOND TREE
(Self portrait. Myself and Verona, my dog)

"See how the farmer waits for the precious fruit of the earth," *WIDOW OF MOAB* "waiting patiently until it receives the early and latter rain."

WIDOW OF MOAB

The reapers and the remnant
Glean and gather
Barley and wheat
The Lord of the harvest

The book of Ruth
Revelation 14:14-16
James 5:7-8
John 4:35
Luke 10:2
Mark 4:26-29
Matthew 3:12
Matthew 13:37-39
Luke 16:22-23
Isaiah 40:6
Job 5:26
Amos 7:1
Psalm 37:2
Jeremiah 9:22
Joel 3:13
Job 34:14-15

"Entreat me not to leave you,
Or to turn back from following after you;
For wherever you go, I will go;
And wherever you lodge, I will lodge;
Your people shall be my people,
And your God, my God.
Where you die, I will die,
And there will I be buried.
The Lord do so to me, and more also,
If anything but death parts you and me."

The reaping of His harvest. Men will be cut down like the grass. Like the prophets and the apostles of the Lamb, we follow Him into persecution and martydom. This is beautiful. A death to death through death itself. And for those in Christ, this is a door to glory. I believe this is right, because death puts love and pride on trial. It tests whether God or the satan is in our hearts. How do we respond? Do we shake our fist and accuse the creator? Do we question His judgment? Does the pride of our heart say that we are more righteous than He, and we would do differently? Or do we respond in humility, meekness and love? Do we step into eternity through the blood of Jesus Christ? Do we respond like our savior and say to our persecutors,
"Father, forgive them, for they do not know what they do."

REAPERS

Jeremiah 9:20-22

THE TOMB AS A WOMB

When you get everything you want
What's left except a bullet in the head
Or a bed made for the dead
The red satin cloth
The coffin box
All the treasures that you sought
They cannot follow you to hell
Or float up through the heavens

We don't make a special emphasis
Of all the so-called blemishes
And impurities of the moon
But we rejoice inside her light
As she unveils her face at night
As a bride before her groom

And why is the womb built as a tomb
To hold the baby at rest
To hold the body at death
And why is a bride beautified for the groom
Adorned with the best
Until the dead resurrect

REAPERS

Are we growing barley?
Are we growing wheat?
And what of this harvest, Lord?
Should I fetch the rod?
Should I grab the sickle?
Threshing the grain of my floor
Is winter approaching?
And what of the spring?
And the heat of the summer again
A body of bondage
A grant of release
To give up the ghost and the breath
And what of the clock
When it ceases ticking?
And what of the lamp going out?
Will I begin to ascend through the heavens
As the mourners lower me down?
For the reaper has come to my door
Knocking with sickle in hand
It would be wise if I would close my eyes
And welcome him as a friend
To have my house in all ways put in order
And my floors always kept swept and clean
Leave your shoes in the street, wipe the dirt from your feet
And let us travel beyond but a dream

My God, my God
I saw a torch in the woods
Like the smoldering bush
Like an eternal flame in the heart
My God, my God
I see a glimmer of hope
At this death on a rope
At the songs growing dim in the dark
My God, my God
I heard the voice of a man
I heard Elijah again
I heard shouting, "off with his head!"
Wisdom calls to the wiser
John the Baptizer
Will come telling all to repent

www.ingramcontent.com/pod-product-compliance
Lightning Source LLC
Chambersburg PA
CBHW041819080526
44587CB00004B/139